THE LIFE & TIMES OF
GRACE KELLY

D1577582

THE LIFE & TIMES OF

Grace Kelly

BY
Penny Stempel

‖‖·PARRAGON·‖‖

This edition first published by
Parragon Book Service Ltd in 1996

Parragon Book Service Ltd
Unit 13–17 Avonbridge Trading Estate
Atlantic Road, Avonmouth
Bristol BS11 9QD

Produced by Magpie Books,
an imprint of Robinson Publishing

Cover picture courtesy of Aquarius Picture Library

Illustrations courtesy of: Hulton Deutsch Collection;
London Features International; Mirror Syndication
International; Peter Newark's Pictures

ISBN 0 75251 547 0

A copy of the British Library Cataloguing in Publication
Data is available from the British Library.

Typeset by Whitelaw & Palmer Ltd, Glasgow
Printed in Singapore

THE BRICKLAYER'S DAUGHTER

Grace Kelly, American princess. The convent girl from Philadelphia with the cool, classical good looks won the hearts of the American people as star of the silver screen. Then she won the heart of her Prince and became Princess of Monaco. But this fairytale was not all sugar: beneath Grace's elegant and impeccable exterior lay the spice of a sensual woman whose lovers included Hollywood's greatest leading men. And there was no

Grace Kelly

picture-book ending to this story: Grace Kelly met a tragic death on the perilous mountain roads of the French Riviera at the age of only 52. To this day the facts of the fatal car accident remain uncertain.

Grace Kelly was in many ways the product of her family background, inheriting the striking good looks of her parents and driven her whole life long by the need for her father's approval – for Jack Kelly it was not enough for his children to succeed, they had to excel.

Jack Kelly was born in 1890, one of a large Irish Catholic family of ten children living in the immigrant quarter of East Falls, Philadelphia. His first job was as a bricklayer, but soon he started his own business, 'Kelly for Brickwork'. With Jack Kelly at the helm the firm could not fail and Jack became a millionaire.

But it was in sport that Jack Kelly's ambition and grit really showed through, and his rowing skills on the single sculls gave him the status of a hero in Philadelphia. In 1919, at the age of 29, he won every race he entered, including the US singles sculling championship. His application to compete in the Diamond Sculls at the Henley Royal Regatta, however, was rejected – because he earned his living from manual labour. But in 1920 he won the Gold Medal at the Olympic Games in Belgium, putting the Englishman who won the Diamond Sculls in second place.

When Grace was born on 12 November 1929 she entered a world of privilege and luxury. The family lived in a three-storey, 17-room brick mansion built by Kelly's own firm high on a hill above Philadelphia, an address – 3901 Henry Avenue – to aspire to. The family

Kelly was a playwright who in 1926 had won the Pulitzer Prize for his play *Craig's Wife*. At one time a big name on Broadway, his work had also taken him to Hollywood where four of his plays were made into films starring such screen legends as Joan Crawford and Spencer Tracy. Her dear Uncle Walter was a renowned vaudeville comedian, while Aunt Grace, who sadly died before her namesake was born, was a comic actress and mimic. When the time came, the aspiring young actress could point out to her father proof within his own family that the stage could lead to success. (It was, after all, a loan from his well-off showbiz brothers, Walter and George, that financed Jack Kelly's business venture.) And the mere mention of Uncle George's name was also to open an all-important door to the would-be young thespian's acting career.

Until she was 13, Grace Kelly was schooled by the Catholic Sisters of the Academy of the Assumption, Ravenshill, Philadelphia; here she learned her catechism and how to behave and dress with respect and decorum. She also learned an unshakeable belief in the Catholic faith which was never to leave her and was to be an important factor in her marriage to His Serene Highness, Prince Rainier of Monaco.

If Grace was perceived by her teachers as a good and proper girl, her classmates could tell a different tale. They knew a girl prone to the giggles, who had a mischievous and adventurous side and would happily join others smoking forbidden cigarettes behind the convent grotto. A more mature Grace would prove just as capable of savouring forbidden fruit of a more sensual flavour.

Such rebellious behaviour was certainly not encouraged at the Stevens School in Germantown at which Grace's education was completed. Here, in a wood-panelled mansion, under the tutelage of Miss Susie Stevens, Grace learned such essential life skills as etiquette. During her time here Grace began her self-education in matters of love and dating. It was not an auspicious start. At 14 she showed little sign of the swan who would later emerge from the plump, bespectacled teenager (she would always be short-sighted), concerned at the small size of her breasts and suffering from a nasal voice which would later require substantial work to pave her way to her chosen career. But barely a year later Grace's sense of fun, her wonderful complexion and fine features came into their own.

Grace Kelly

She had also already chosen her future path. Roles in school plays, the influence of beloved Uncle George and a trip to a production by local amateur dramatic company, the Old Academy Players, together fired young Grace's determination. First she ensured that she had her father's – albeit reluctant – consent, then she set about putting her plan into action. In 1942, at the age of 12, she made her stage debut in *Don't Feed the Animals* with the Old Academy Players and soon she was a company stalwart. Her commitment, punctuality and professionalism made her a welcome member of the troupe.

During 1944, as Grace's career path gently progressed in the background, romance blossomed in the foreground. Grace's first serious relationship was with Charles Harper Davis, a schoolfriend of her brother Kell's, the son of the local Buick dealer – it was also the first of many to be abruptly ended at the bidding of her strong-minded father. When Kelly heard that after graduation Harper Davis would be enlisting in the navy, the spectre of hasty marriage rose in his mind. Harper Davis was not at all the son-in-law Jack wished for. In the same way that was to perplex and even infuriate her later lovers, Grace gave in without question to her father's will. Within two days, without giving any reason, she ended the romance.

Over the next few years Grace had several regular boyfriends, and was a much-loved and popular date. Not only was she good fun and good company, she was also surprisingly unselfconscious when it came to sexual experimentation. She remained a virgin until shortly before leaving home for college, but in the meantime the young men lucky enough to date her found her a carefree partner, confident in and comfortable with her sexual appeal.

Grace enjoyed a few playful years while she finished her schooling. Her graduation from Stevens School in the summer of 1947 coincided with an altogether more significant event in the Kelly family calendar – brother Kell's bid to win the supreme prize – the Diamond Sculls at Henley. On 5 July 1947, aged only 20, Kell achieved his family's ambition and restored his father's honour. Now, albeit belatedly, Grace's career could receive a little attention.

ACADEMY TO
TELEVISION

Grace wanted to attend one of the leading
private drama schools in the United States,
the American Academy of Arts. Situated
above Carnegie Hall in New York, its past
pupils included Kirk Douglas, Spencer Tracy,
Katherine Hepburn and Lauren Bacall.
Grace's aunt Marie Magee, a one-time
actress, was duly enlisted to help. But it was
too late. On enquiry Marie Magee was
informed that all the places were filled and

registration was closed. It was now that Uncle George Kelly's name came to the rescue. On 20 August Grace was given an audition; next to her name in the record book were written the words 'niece of George Kelly'. This is not to say that Grace did not have talent: the notes also declared Grace to be a 'lovely child' with 'good and promising youthful symptoms'. In all likelihood, they predicted, she 'should develop well'.

The American Academy of Dramatic Arts was the conservative choice for an aspiring actor. At a time when the daring new 'Method' acting favoured by the likes of Brando was all the rage, the solid, old-fashioned craft methods favoured by white-haired German Jew Charles Jehlinger, director of instruction since 1890, seemed to belong to a past age. But Grace had chosen a milieu which ideally suited her. Bohemian it may have been, but at the Academy proper dress, etiquette and behaviour were as important as they were to Grace.

Next to her cool, demure-seeming exterior, Grace's pure, clear tones came to be regarded as one of her assets. The Academy employed a voice coach, Aristide d'Angelo, who together with Englishman Edward Goodman was in charge of eradicating all errors of pro-nunciation. Dialect of any kind was worked upon mercilessly until the students' tones emulated the Oxbridge accent of their tutors. This was the area in which Grace most needed help and she applied herself to the necessary exercises with typical diligence, to be rewarded with a clear, high-class accent. In addition to her Academy lessons, she took private tuition from Mario Fiorella, an operatic tenor, and spent long hours alone practising the methods she had been shown. Now she sounded as elegant as she looked.

She lodged in an establishment suitable for young ladies, with thespian connections. Joan Crawford and Gene Tierney were two of many illustrious past inhabitants of the Barbizon Hotel for Women at Sixty-third Street and Lexington, which required three references and forbade male visitors above the ground floor.

This did not, however, inhibit Grace's romantic progress. In reality the Barbizon did little to enforce its rules and its reputation only added to the attractions of its inmates. Grace was very soon involved with handsome fellow student Herbie Miller. The two worked at their voice exercises and viewed the latest

European art movies together. Their friendship led directly to Grace's first magazine cover: one day she accompanied Herbie on one of his modelling assignments, and no sooner had they arrived than the photographer asked if he could take Grace's picture. The result made the cover of *Redbook* magazine. In the following year, Grace adorned the covers of *True Romance*, *True Story* and *Cosmopolitan*, as well as providing visual appeal for the campaigns of products as diverse as cigarettes, toothpaste, beer and insecticide. She even posed for lingerie advertisements, until the Sisters at her old school gently expressed their disapproval. Grace had fallen into a life as a model, and it was already clear that the camera loved her. The work was lucrative, but Grace kept a clear head. Her first priority was to repay her father for all her tuition and accommodation bills. Only when which was repeatedly to captivate the men in her life and to provide her unique appeal on the big screen: Grace the modest, Grace the elegant – but the suspicion that, once stirred, it could be Grace the wild and reckless.

Grace and D'Arcy parted on good terms when the actor left for work in Paris. The next affair was to be deeper-felt, more lasting and more important. It also brought about a severe conflict between Grace and her parents. It was the winter of 1948, Grace was 19 and in the second and final year of her course at the Academy. The acting group she was allotted to was supervised by young director Don Richardson. Aged only 30, Richardson – who had changed his name from Melvin Schwartz – already had a string of professional credits to his name. He was dark-haired, dark-eyed, intense and charismatic.

The reserved blonde girl in his class did not stand out particularly until she burst into tears one evening when a classmate played a prank on her. Taking it upon himself to comfort his distressed student, her tutor found himself out in the freezing snow trying in vain to hail Grace a taxi. When all else failed, he invited her to warm up in his apartment nearby. By the end of the evening they were lovers. Richardson and Grace fell head over heels in love and she spent most Saturday nights at Richardson's scruffy bachelor flat although, always the good Catholic, she would also slip out of bed on the Sunday morning and attend church.

Richardson was quick to recognize that Grace was looking for a father figure to replace Jack Kelly's influence in her life and he was happy to play her Svengali. Realizing her future lay in the movies, he took her along to meet Eddie van Cleve, a powerful agent at MCA. Van Cleve was enchanted with the young actress. Grace now had an agent.

In the spring of 1949 the unfortunate suitor found himself on his way to Philadelphia to meet the Kellys. He was not hopeful – he was, after all, Jewish, and in the process of a divorce. But he was unprepared for their chilling reception. The family made no secret of their feelings: there were Jewish jokes, an invitation to their Catholic church service, and laughter and ridicule at Richardson's prediction that Grace would be a star. While Richardson was required to admire Jack Kelly's buildings and sports trophies, the family had no comprehension of theatre or culture of any kind. And when Margaret

Kelly discovered in the hapless guest's belongings a letter detailing his divorce proceedings, Richardson was ordered from the house. Within fifteen minutes he was on his way back to New York, alone.

Grace, meanwhile, was forbidden to return to New York until the winter, when she won a prestigious part in Strindberg's *The Father* which was due to play on Broadway, and was reluctantly allowed to go. She returned to New York, and to Don Richardson. This time the Kellys' disapproval came in the form of bribes and threats administered to her lover. Once again Grace remained passive in the face of her family's behaviour and the relationship petered out.

Next came 40-year-old Claudius Charles Philippe, Banqueting Manager of the Waldorf-

Astoria Hotel, strong-willed, charming and legendary in New York café society - and twice-divorced. Once again the two wanted to marry, once again Jack Kelly vetoed the match.

Then Grace was wined, dined and proposed to by a suitor just about acceptable to her parents – 30-year-old Mohammed Reza Pahlavi, Shah of Iran, on an official visit to the States, danced night after night until the early hours with Miss Kelly. But Grace, while accepting his exquisite gifts turned down his proposal. A lifetime in Iran would, she felt, hinder her career.

Grace acquitted herself well enough in her Broadway debut, *The Father*, but the play closed after a few months and she was left with an endless round of unfruitful auditions. Then came the new medium of television which suited her style better; soon she was a regular performer in the live plays that the emerging networks were beginning to broadcast. She was in good company. It was to television that all the young and exciting talent was finding its way and stars such as Lee Remick, James Dean, Steve McQueen, Walter Matthau and Charles Bronson were also appearing on the small screen.

Between 1950 and 1953 Grace appeared in over 60 television shows, averaging more than one a month. But every summer she returned to the Bucks County Playhouse for work in summer stock (equivalent to Britain's repertory); while playing in Colorado, Grace received, on 10 August 1951, a telegram from Hollywood. It was from movie producer

High Noon

Stanley Kramer and it read: 'Can you report August 28, lead opposite Gary Cooper. Tentative title *High Noon*.'

THE BIG SCREEN

Grace's first taste of Hollywood had been in the summer of 1950 when she appeared briefly as a 'lady in lawyer's office' in a film titled *Fourteen Hours*. She had turned down the resulting offers of long-term studio contracts. She was not in need of money thanks to her modelling work and Uncle George had always impressed upon her that to accept such a contract was to sell one's soul and surrender all control.

Thus she was available to the heavyweight,

independent team of Stanley Kramer, producer; Carl Foreman, writer; and Fred Zinnemann, director, to play the marshal's young Quaker wife opposite Gary Cooper in *High Noon*. It was a pivotal role and it went to Grace because Kramer could only afford to use a complete unknown. When she arrived to meet her director wearing her customary white gloves she looked to Zinnemann the very image of the part she was to play – the Quaker girl from the East arriving among the wild people of the West.

The shooting of *High Noon* took only 28 days, and even if Gary Cooper had not been suffering from woman troubles and ill health, there would have been little chance of an affair. On the instructions of her mother, Grace was chaperoned throughout the shoot by 18-year-old Lizanne.

director Gregory Ratoff who wanted Grace to screen-test for a part in his film *Taxi* which was in pre-production with Twentieth Century-Fox. The part was that of a simple, immigrant Irish girl and Grace thoroughly prepared herself for the task by asking an Irish friend to read to her. Ratoff was keen to cast her, but Fox preferred to economize and use one of their own contract actresses. Her screen test was also seen by director John Ford, however, and it led to a part in a far bigger movie playing opposite major stars. Ford had been hired by MGM for *Mogambo*, a remake of the early thirties hit *Red Dust*. It was to be shot on location in East Africa and the leading man was none other than Clark Gable. Grace was offered third billing after Gable and Ava Gardner and, even attached to a seven-year contract, it was an offer that Grace couldn't refuse. She did not, however,

surrender easily. In her clear-headed way, she
had worked out her conditions for signing on
the dotted line: she would continue to live in
New York, she would be committed to no
more three pictures a year and she would still
be free to work in theatre should she so wish.
MGM agreed and Grace became a contract
player.

By November 1952 Grace was in Nairobi,
where she and her legendary leading man
were soon lost in romance. It was the ideal
setting for Grace to indulge the wild side of
her nature, and for Gable – at 28 years her
senior, yet another surrogate father in her
love-life – it was a pleasure to dally with a
beautiful young co-star. Others in the cast
reported that the pair, inseparable throughout
the shoot, made no secret of their romance.
They soon paid the penalty. Not only were

the papers full of the love-affair, but worse, the reports prompted action from Grace's mother. While the company were in London for the final month's shoot, Margaret Kelly arrived to chaperone her all-too susceptible daughter. Gable soon eased the relationship into friendship – a transition which the young actress found more difficult than he did. She could, however, take some comfort from the fact that her performance in *Mogambo* led to *Look* magazine declaring her Best Actress of 1953, and the greater honour in the same year of an Academy Award nomination as Best Supporting Actress.

Grace Kelly had been noticed in Hollywood. Her cool beauty and poise together with the hint of deeper passion intrigued movie-goers worldwide – and fascinated the director who was to produce Grace's most memorable and accomplished performances. Her next role was for Alfred Hitchcock, and the film was *Dial M for Murder*.

Hitchcock famously described Grace Kelly as a 'snow-covered volcano' and he exploited the qualities he had so accurately glimpsed in her to the full in this part. In the movie, a detective thriller, Grace placed Margo Wendice, the female lead and, indeed, only female part. Unhappy in her marriage, Margo falls in love with a visiting American writer but is found out by her husband (Ray Milland) who engages an assassin to murder her. His plot fails, and Margot stabs her assailant in a violent struggle. Hitchcock knew that with an actress such as this he could afford to be more overtly erotic and in the murder scene he had Grace, dressed in a nightgown, writhe, moan and thrash her bare

legs in a sensual and meticulously choreo-
graphed performance.

It was not only her director who appreciated
Grace's barely concealed sexuality on the set.
All the men fell for her, including the writer
and her co-stars. But once again it was her
leading man who won her favours. Dark
haired, smooth-mannered, Oscar winner Ray
Milland was twice Grace's age and married;
even so, they made no attempt to conceal
their romance. Lizanne, sent again by Mama
to chaperone Grace, was forced to abandon
her efforts as her sisters' flat filled up with
Milland's bouquets. Inevitably the papers got
hold of the story and not all handled it with
caution. Milland's wife, Mal, was not amused.
But she was a strong woman and she issued
her husband with an ultimatum. He went
back to her, leaving Grace wounded and

regretful. Leading lady or not, at 23 Grace did not have the sophistication to deal with Hollywood's seasoned players. She had believed that Milland's marriage was over, and she had thought that she was special, not just one of many.

She may have felt emotionally bruised, but Grace had now truly arrived in Hollywood and was in such demand that she next had to choose between two hugely prestigious scripts. It was a difficult choice. One was Alfred Hitchcock's next film, *Rear Window*. Once again it would be a murder mystery. Temporarily confined to a wheelchair by an accident, a young photographer (James Stewart), to while away the boredom, uses his telephoto lens to spy on the apartments opposite. The events he sees unfold lead him to believe that a murder has taken place. He

Rear Window

tells his girlfriend, and together they set out to investigate the suspected murder.

The other project, however, could have broken new ground for Grace and was both challenging and demanding. The film was the raw and harsh *On the Waterfront*, which was to win an Oscar for the young Marlon Brando.

Grace, wisely, went for known territory and a director who understood the nuances of her appeal. She chose to play smart, sophisticated Lisa Fremont in the Greenwich village-set *Rear Window*. She was repaid by Hitchcock's devoting his attention to every detail of her dress and performance. The two developed an understanding that was to grow into a warm, long-term friendship, sharing as they did a superficial reserve which hid deeper undercurrents. Grace trusted the authoritarian director sufficiently to allow him to draw out her usually hidden depths of fun-loving sensuality. As a result, *Rear Window* showcased Grace Kelly at her very best, encapsulating her appeal on the big screen. The film was a box-office sensation when it opened in the summer of 1954.

Next came a movie with the Oscar-winning director–producer partnership of William Perlberg and George Seaton with whom Grace started work on *The Bridges at Toko-Ri* at the end of 1953. In the film, based on James Michener's documentary novel of the Korean War, Grace was cast alongside William Holden – aged 35, strikingly handsome and a renowned flirt and heart-throb. *The Bridges at Toko-Ri* was a daring and explicit film by the standards of its times. It was the first to show Grace Kelly in a bathing suit and the only one to show her in bed with a man: she and Holden were featured in neat pyjamas, perched primly on opposite sides of the bed. The scene was nonetheless considered risqué.

Far more scandalous was the couple's off-screen relationship. Although he was in fact married to actress Ardi Ankerson Gaine, the dutiful daughter took her new partner home to meet Daddy and, unsurprisingly, the meeting was no more successful than Grace's previous attempts. The affair limped to a quiet, natural end.

The Bridges at Toko-Ri did little to advance Grace's career. Her appearance was a brief interlude in what was essentially a war movie. But it did lead to a part in the next Perlberg–Seaton collaboration, *The Country*

Girl, a film based on Clifford Odet's massive Broadway hit of 1950. The female lead had a rare strong role as the ground-down but still tough wife of a once-great actor, who has hit the depths and become an alcoholic. And it was this role, so different from all Grace Kelly's others, that was to win her an Oscar.

It was also to bring her a suitor to her parents' liking. Bing Crosby was playing opposite Grace and, at the age of 50, still recovering from his wife's recent death after a difficult marriage, Bing proved no more immune to Grace's charms than any other of her leading men. This was a respectable courtship – Bing after all was a bona fide widower and a practising Catholic who took Grace to church on a Sunday. But this was not the man Grace wished to marry.

For the loan of Grace Kelly to play *The Country Girl*, Paramount had paid MGM $50,000, and Grace had had to agree to play in one of MGM's studio potboilers, *Green Fire*. But no sooner was this shoot over than she forced MGM to release her for her fifth loan-out in only eight months and the fourth time to Paramount. Grace was determined – it was for another Hitchcock film and she would be playing opposite Cary Grant. Paramount paid up another $50,000 and loaned MGM William Holden, one of their own top stars, and Grace got to play the part she wanted in the great director's *To Catch a Thief*.

To Catch a Thief was to shoot in the South of France and before she left, Grace, as always, made careful preparations, taking French lessons, and writing to one of her

Grace Kelly

would-be suitors to follow her to Paris. This was Oleg Loiewski-Cassini, couturier to the best of Manhattan society, later Jackie Kennedy's favoured designer. He was charming, persistent and a gourmet of beautiful women.

Grace played a rich girl who, on holiday with her mother, falls for and pursues a debonair Riviera jewel thief played by Cary Grant. It was a spicy part with plenty of verbal sparring and double entendres and Grace was allowed to be both saucy and sexual, planting a memorably passionate kiss on Grant's lips. It took Grace's appeal one step further and was another classic Hitchcock–Kelly collaboration.

Grace fell in love with the South of France and she also fell in love with Loiewski-

Cassini. On their return to the States there was the obligatory confrontation with her family with the usual outcome, Grace as always staying silent during her family's harsh treatment of her lover.

The County Girl was released in December 1954 to rapturous critical acclaim and Grace won unanimous plaudits. She had shown that she could act with passion and perception. The New York Drama Critics' Circle nominated Grace Best Actress of 1954. Now she was tipped for the Oscars the following spring.

The competition was fierce. Grace's rivals for Best Actress included Audrey Hepburn (*Sabrina*) and Judy Garland (*A Star is Born*). Audrey Hepburn had won Best Actress the year before for *Roman Holiday* but the talented and charismatic Judy Garland, surprisingly, had never yet won and many were backing her.

By a curious coincidence the star selected to announce Grace's category at the awards ceremony on 30 March 1955 was her past love, William Holden, whose pleasure was evident as he announced her name as the winner. Grace, called upon for her speech, was only able to tell her audience, 'The thrill of this moment prevents me from saying exactly what I feel', before bursting into tears.

But even now the all-important approval from Grace's father was not forthcoming. His response, reproduced by papers around the world was, as ever, brutally frank. 'I simply can't believe Grace won,' he told

In Cannes for the 1955 Film Festival

reporters. 'Of the four children, she's the last one I'd expected to support me in my old age.'

THE PRINCE

As an Oscar-winning star, Grace Kelly was invited to head the American delegation to the Cannes Film Festival and in May 1955 she returned to the French Riviera. There she found an old lover, Jean-Pierre Aumont, with whom she enjoyed a new and carefree romance. She also attended a photo-opportunity which was to change her life for ever.

Just along the coast from Cannes lies the

Principality of Monaco, a tiny and unique mini-state less than one square mile in size. Ruled by the Grimaldi princes since the thirteenth century, its inhabitants lived clustered around a picturesque harbour. On one side, at the top of a steep road up the rock, stands the palace and on the other, are the world famous Monte Carlo casino and the glistening white Hôtel de Paris.

Presiding over this fairy-tale fiefdom was His Serene Highness Prince Rainier III. Then aged 31 and still a bachelor the prince was coming under pressure to find himself a wife. Monaco depended on the rich and famous of the world to patronize its casino, use its address as tax exiles or launder their money in its banks. The Principality was in danger of losing its glamour and glitz and, more seriously, its special status if Rainier produced no heir.

On 6 May 1955, Rainier and Grace Kelly met for the first time. The occasion, set up by *Paris Match* journalist Pierre Galante, began inauspiciously. A strike by France's electrical workers meant Grace could not dry her hair or wear her intended dress, the photographers' car ran into theirs, and was an hour late. But the portly prince and the blonde actress were not unaffected by each other's charm. In keeping with her good manners Grace wrote to thank the prince. He in turn wrote her a letter, and a correspondence started which was to lead to their marriage.

It was just over six months later, Christmas 1955, that the two met again, This time Rainier visited Grace at her home: unknown to her, Edie and Russ Austin, brash family friends, had contacted the prince's palace when on their European tour, for help in obtaining tickets to Monaco's famous Red Cross Ball. Their request had landed on the desk of Rainier's personal chaplain, Father Francis Tucker who made it his business to further his prince's interests. He supplied the desired tickets and Edie and Russ in return furnished the prince with an invitation to the Kelly Christmas party.

Late on Christmas Day 1955, Prince Rainier arrived at 3901 Henry Avenue, Philadelphia, together with Father Tucker and his personal physician Dr Robert Donat. A prince, never married, with a pedigree some seven centuries old and Roman Catholic – the Grimaldi family had long had a close relationship with the Vatican – must surely please Grace's father. The chaplain's presence guaranteed Jack Kelly's approval. Rainier, meanwhile, was charming, debonair and attentive. Margaret Kelly adeptly invited the prince to spend the night and Grace's older sister Peggy took the prince, the doctor and Grace to her house where the four played cards – in two rooms, Peggy with the doctor. Meanwhile Father Tucker acquired Jack Kelly's permission for the marriage of his second daughter to Prince Rainier III of Monaco. Grace's fate was sealed. At last she had fallen in love with someone 'suitable' – that her father had started life as a manual worker does not seem to have bothered Father Tucker, a fellow Irishman.

There were, of course, conditions attached to the marriage of the prince and the movie star. Grace had to agree to the 'Separation des biens', an agreement stipulating that neither would have any rights over the other's

Grace and Rainier's wedding, 1956

property. This was no hardship since Grace came with a major shareholding in her father's firm. Kelly also had to pay a dowry for the privilege of his daughter marrying a Grimaldi. But perhaps the harshest part of the contract was the requirement that in the event of a divorce, for dynastic reasons, any children would remain in the father's custody. None of these things clouded Grace's happiness. She was a rich woman in her own right and besides had no intention of divorcing Rainier.

Between the marriage announcement and the wedding in April 1956, Grace played one last glittering Hollywood role, in MGM's *High Society*, with music by Cole Porter. She was acting with such musical legends as Frank Sinatra, Bing Crosby, and Louis Armstrong but, undaunted, she took singing lessons and insisted on performing her own songs. She was rewarded for her work when her rendition of 'True Love' went platinum. This was the last trophy the silver screen was to win her. There was no place for the movies in her next role as princess and when Rainier was asked by he press whether his fiancée would star in films again, his reply was 'I don't think so'.

The filming of *High Society* ended on 6 March. On 4 April the USS *Constitution* left the port of New York with great fanfare bearing Grace Kelly, her family and friends to Monaco. On the morning of 12 April the liner approached Monaco's harbour to be met by Prince Rainier III on his yacht. The civil wedding required by Monagesque law took place on Wednesday 18 April and was followed by an extravagant garden party in

The bride and bridegroom drive from the cathedral

the palace grounds for the 3000 adult citizens of Monaco. The religious marriage took place in the cathedral the next day. Grace's wedding dress, designed by Helen Rose, was a gift from MGM. It contained 25 yards of silk, 25 yards of silk-taffeta, 98 yards of silk tulle and over 300 yards of Valenciennes lace. She looked exquisite. After a reception for more than 600 guests in the palace courtyard, Grace and Rainier said their farewells and drove through the palace gate down from the rock, past the cheering crowds, to Rainier's yacht which waited below. The honeymoon was spent cruising round the island of Corsica, visiting its deserted coves and beaches. When they returned at the end of May Grace had already fulfilled her most important duty. She was pregnant.

At 9.27 a.m. on 23 January 1957, nine

months and four days after her wedding day, Grace gave birth to Caroline Louise Marguerite. A national holiday was declared in Monaco. Fourteen months later, on 14 March 1958, she gave birth to a boy, Albert Louis Pierre, son and heir to Rainier. The young family spent many idyllic hours in their private retreat in Provence, Roc Agel, an isolated farmhouse set in a 60-acre estate high in the hills above Monaco. The old, stone-walled building was home to Rainier's metal workshop and big band drum kit and Grace's mementoes of her Hollywood years.

But as in the best fairytales, it was not all sunshine. The princess had to put a brave face on dark and unhappy moments. For some time after her arrival she found it impossible to make her mark on the time-honoured ways of the castle, and the gloomy palace employed a cook, a secretary, a bevy of maids and a chauffeur/gardener. And life was not just comfortable, it was packed with pleasure. There was a panelled cellar equipped as a bar, a tennis court which was flooded to provide an ice rink each winter, and a huge metal container (used for mixing cement in) delivered every year by 'Kelly for Brickwork', which filled with water, was the scene of bathing frolics during the hot months of the year.

Grace was the third of four children. In 1924 Kelly had married Margaret Majer, the beautiful blonde daughter of German immigrants. Their first child, Peggy, was born in September 1925, Jack Jr. ('Kell') was born in May 1927 and the baby of the family, Lizanne, arrived in June 1933. It is often the case that siblings' relative merits appear one way within the home setting and quite differently to outsiders. Grace may have grown up to be the golden-girl-next-door for the whole of the United States, but at 3901 Henry Avenue she always came last. Her father openly admitted that the beautiful, vivacious and sporty Peggy was his favourite; brother Kell took up the baton from his father, toiled, sweated and strove at the single sculls, and succeeded in rescuing family honour by winning the Diamond Sculls at Henley; and the strong-minded and robust Lizanne was the bubbly and beloved baby.

Grace, on the other hand, was quiet, reserved and prone to colds and illness. She would spend hours alone playing with her dolls. But those who felt sorry for her then, as in later life, would find that this was a young girl with unexpected strength and self-sufficiency. A favourite family anecdote tells how, in a fit of

HER SERENE HIGHNESS

Grace applied her usual grit, optimism and determination to her work as Princess of Monaco and used her position to further causes she believed in. She became a strong-minded spokeswoman for the La Leche League which promotes breast-feeding; she called a halt to Monaco's famous annual pigeon shoot, declaring it a barbaric event; she organized an annual Christmas party at the palace for every Monagesque child between 3 and 12, and a tea party every

A family holiday in Switzerland, 1963

Christmas season for the elderly and infirm at which each of them was given a gift. She was a frequent visitor to local homes for the elderly, to the orphanage and to the Princess Grace Hospital, opened in 1958 and named after her. She helped found a day-care centre for the children of working mothers and she used her presidency of the Monaco Red Cross to make sure that its annual ball attracted stars of the calibre of David Niven, Cary Grant and Frank Sinatra. In the early sixties she was a founder member of AMADE, L'Association Mondiale des Amis de l'Enfance – the World Association of Friends of Children.

She involved herself in her Principality's cultural affairs as well and started an annual ballet festival. When Monaco's redevelopment fever threatened to run amok and

Princess Grace, 1971

demolish the most beautiful of Monte Carlo's buildings, Grace's personal intervention successfully blocked the destruction of the elegant Hermitage Hotel. She also famously befriended the black singer and dancer Josephine Baker, rescuing her and her many adopted children from financial ruin by organizing repayment of their debts.

The early sixties were to test Grace's strength and resolve. On 20 June 1960, when Grace was 30, her father died from cancer of the stomach. She herself suffered two miscarriages after Albert's birth in 1958, which deeply saddened her. She began to sleep for long hours during the day. A glimmer of hope arose in the corpulent shape of Alfred Hitchcock, only to be cruelly dashed. Grace was to star in Hitchcock's new film, *Marnie*, due to shoot in the summer of 1962. But no sooner was the public announcement made than the gossip columns of the USA gave full vent to their notion that if she wished to return to Hollywood the Princess of Monaco must be unhappy in her marriage. It was not the case, and Rainier had backed her plans. But Grace withdrew from the project and Tippi Hedren took her place. Now, however, it was clear that she would not return to the film studios again.

On 1 February 1965 Grace at last gave birth to Princess Stephanie Marie Elisabeth, the third child she had hoped for for so long. But by 1966, after ten years continually in thrall to her husband's moods and boredom, she was far from happy in her marriage. And she was dealt another shattering blow in July 1967. Aged 37 and two months' pregnant, Grace was in London with her family when she was

Christmas presents for the children of Monaco, 1967

rushed to hospital; the baby boy she was carrying was dead. There could, the doctors told her, be no more pregnancies.

Grace Kelly never stayed depressed for long and from her mid-forties she began to tread a new path in a marriage whose partners increasingly went their separate ways. She now worried about her looks and her weight but she never lost her immense charm and zest for life. She began to spend more and more time in Paris and she developed friendships with a coterie of younger men. There was Robert Dornhelm, a film director aged 30, Romanian by birth and Austrian by nationality whom Grace met in 1976 when he filmed the introduction she gave to a documentary on the Russian Imperial Ballet School. They maintained a close relationship from then on, planning and collaborating on

Family portrait, 1974

other projects. One of these was *Rearranged*, a filmed tale of mistaken identity starring Princess Grace as herself and set in her Monaco garden club.

Her relationship with Dornhelm was central to her middle years, but there were others: a young Swedish actor, Per Mattsson, whom she invited to her hotel room to play the piano and sing duets; Jim McMullen, a New York restauranteur in his late twenties who was a frequent guest of Grace's for six years; and Jeffory Martin FitzGerald, a tall, handsome, 29-year-old business executive whom she met on a Concorde trip and who was almost certainly her lover.

One of Grace's newly discovered interests in these years was poetry. In 1976, she was invited to read at a poetry recital at the

Princess Grace and Prince Albert, 1976

Edinburgh Festival, with the theme of the American Bicentennial. Her four recitals were an unqualified success and she began travelling regularly to perform in poetry recitals from Vienna to London to Dublin. The project closest to her heart in these years, however, was the creation of her own theatre overlooking Monaco harbour. It was converted from a convention hall to Grace's detailed specifications and it opened in December 1981, in the presence of theatrical luminaries such as Dirk Bogarde.

Grace had plenty of need for distraction. Not only did her marriage lack passion but her daughters, famously spoilt and wilful, were increasingly causing her problems. Far from emulating their mother's elegant and dignified public performance, the sisters constantly pursued unsuitable relationships and gave rise to scandal greedily circulated by the media of the world. And unlike their mother in her youth the two princesses refused to bow to the will of their parents. At 19 Caroline began to date Philippe Junot, a famous ladies' man 17 years her senior. After a year she gave her mother an ultimatum – if she was not allowed to marry Junot she would run off and live with him. The couple wed in June 1978 and divorced in October 1980.

Stephanie, meanwhile, at 17 fell in love with Paul Belmondo, the 19-year-old son of actor Jean-Paul Belmondo. First she insisted on holidaying with him in Antigua and then, on her return, she announced that she was throwing in her hard-earned place at the prestigious Institute of Fashion Design in Paris which she was due to take up in five days' time. Paul was going to train as a racing-car driver and Stephanie wished to do the same. Grace was distraught. She could not accept this path for her younger daughter. She persuaded Stephanie to return to Monaco to discuss her plans. Some say these discussions played a part in Grace's tragic, early death.

It was Monday 13 September 1982, a beautiful, sunny day in the South of France. The atmosphere at Roc Agel had been tense for the last few days and now mother and daughter were to drive down into Monaco, talking as they travelled. Grace rarely drove – she was acknowledged to be a poor driver and preferred not to take the wheel since an accident a few years back – but that morning she dismissed the waiting chauffeur and she and Stephanie set off alone in the waiting brown Rover.

Princess Grace and her family on holiday, 1978

As they drove down the winding CD37 out of the village of La Turbie and towards the lethal route's sharpest hairpin bends a professional truck driver, Yves Phily, was just behind their car. Suddenly the Rover veered from the centre of the road to the left, its side hitting the rocks of the mountain. Phily sounded his horn and the Rover steadied its course. But as the car approached the next hairpin bend he saw to his horror that, instead of braking, the Rover accelerated and shot forward at high speed. Instead of rounding the sharp curve of the road to the right, the car flew straight ahead and took off into the air.

The Rover sailed on and over a drop of 45 metres slicing the top of a tree in its path. As it plummeted the car hit the trunk of another tree, bounced upside-down onto a pile of rocks, rolled over several times and finally came to rest tilted onto its nose and roof. The passenger door and roof were crushed.

Captain Roger Bencze arrived at the scene at 10.30 a.m., some 35 minutes later, and five minutes after Prince Rainier. The Monaco fire department was already loading the unconscious Grace and the sobbing, hysterical Stephanie into an ambulance to take them to Monaco's Princess Grace Hospital, the nearest to the scene of the crash.

There were witnesses to the crash, and they spoke to Bencze. But the man much quoted in the papers, one Sesto Lequio, had not seen the accident. His claim that Stephanie had been driving was nonetheless headlined by media around the world. Bencze's scrupulous investigation came to a different conclusion. In his opinion, Grace had temporarily lost control of the car and slumped her foot on the accelerator when intending to hit the brake. Members of the Grimaldi family were exempt from questioning or examination by French police officers and so this route of enquiry was closed. Sightings of Grace at the wheel of the Rover between 9.45 a.m. and the time at which the car clock stopped – 9.54 a.m. – supported Bencze's theories. Sabotage was ruled out as a possibility by the report of the professional accident investigator: there was no sign that the vehicle had been tampered with in any way whatsoever.

At Princess Grace Hospital the two passengers – neither of whom had been wearing seat belts – were undergoing examination. Princess Stephanie had suffered only cuts and bruises. Princess Grace had a broken thigh bone, a fracture of the knee and a fracture of the arm. Still unconscious, one of her eyes was not responding to changes in light and this, most serious of all, indicated brain injury. Diagnosis and treatment could not start immediately because, in order that Grace could be put on a mechanical respirator, she had been given a narcotic drug. She could not be given the necessary CAT scan X-ray of the brain until it wore off. Furthermore, because the hospital did not have the necessary equipment, Grace would first have to be taken across town and carried upstairs to a first-floor clinic in which was located Monaco's only CAT scan machine.

The scan, finally possible at midnight, nearly twelve hours after the accident, showed two areas of damage to the brain. One indicated that Grace had suffered a stroke, the other showed traumatic damage to the front of the brain, the result of a physical blow. The doctors attending Grace stated that the stroke had been only a minor one, but that it had caused Grace momentarily to lose consciousness and drive off the road, so causing the second set of injuries to her head.

In fact it could not be proved that the stroke occurred before the accident, or that the head injuries provoked the stroke: the CAT scan could not determine this. Certainly Grace had been complaining of headaches during the previous summer and there was a history of strokes in the Kelly family. Either way, the stroke–before–trauma thesis became the official explanation and it accorded with Bencze's theories.

On Tuesday 14 September 1982, one day after the crash, the senior doctor conferred with Prince Rainier, Caroline and Albert. There was, he said, no more he could do for Grace. There seemed little point extending her life artificially. Her family went into her room to say their last goodbyes and then accepted his advice. At 10.15 p.m. that night her life-support machine was switched off.

The funeral of Her Serene Highness Princess Grace of Monaco was held on the morning of Saturday 18 September, attended by, among others, the Queen of Spain, the King and Queen of Belgium, Madame François Mitterand, Nancy Reagan, Diana, Princess of Wales and Cary Grant. People wept in the streets; Rainier sobbed openly.

The coffin lay in a side chapel of the cathedral for three days and then on Tuesday 21 September Grace was laid to rest in the

Princess Grace

Grimaldi family vault. Tourists — as many as nine thousand a day on a busy weekend — still file past her marble tombstone in the great semicircle of princes and princesses around the high altar.

In her last interview, Grace, Princess of Monaco had said simply, 'I would like to be remembered as a decent human being and a caring one.'

FURTHER MINI SERIES
INCLUDE

THEY DIED TOO YOUNG

Elvis
James Dean
Buddy Holly
Jimi Hendrix
Sid Vicious
Marc Bolan
Ayrton Senna
Marilyn Monroe
Jim Morrison

THEY DIED TOO YOUNG

Malcolm X
Kurt Cobain
River Phoenix
John Lennon
Glenn Miller
Isadora Duncan
Rudolph Valentino
Freddie Mercury
Bob Marley

FURTHER MINI SERIES
INCLUDE

HEROES OF THE WILD WEST

General Custer
Butch Cassidy and the Sundance Kid
Billy the Kid
Annie Oakley
Buffalo Bill
Geronimo
Wyatt Earp
Doc Holliday
Sitting Bull
Jesse James